VOCAL SELECTIONS

Contents

Despite its brilliantly original score and lyrics, a 1964 show, Anyone Can Whistle, closed after nine performances."

That statement was part of the cover story in Newsweek, April 23, 1973, on Stephen Sondheim. It headlined him as "Broadway's Music Man."

The history of Anyone Can Whistle as an on-going musical was limited. It opened at the Majestic Theatre in New York City on April 4, 1964 and closed on April 11, 1964. (It had tried-out at the Forest Theatre in Philadelphia, opening there March 2, 1964.)

The review in the New York Times included the following: . . . Intention is to suggest that the best hope for the world's sanity lies in madness. Toward this goal, it conjures up a town in decay, a powerful mayoress with a crooked henchman, a miracle of having water flow from a rock, a nurse who believes in being scientific and practical and a stranger who is mistaken for a new doctor but who turns out to be a candidate for the community's mental institution."

Anyone Can Whistle was created by Stephen Sondheim (Music and Lyrics) and Arthur Laurents (Book and Direction), their third collaboration. These noted talents had worked together earlier on West Side Story and Gypsy. Anyone Can Whistle was the first musical Mr. Laurents both wrote and directed. It was Mr. Sondheim's second Broadway contribution with both his music and lyrics. (He had contributed only lyrics for West Side Story and Gypsy.)

THE TOWN A town which manufactures exclusively a product that never wears out can only expect eventual financial ruin. From her late husband, officious, attractive Cora Hoover Hooper (Angela Lansbury) has inherited a now-closed factory, the mayoralty of her bankrupt small American town, and the animosity of the townspeople. "They hate me," she complains at the sight of pickets with placards demanding her ouster. The reassurance of Comptroller Schub (Gabriel Dell) that "they hated your husband too," does little to help her solve the immediate problem of how to pay the town's bills without dipping into her own pocketbook, stuffed with the total assets of the town. In Me and My Town, she sings of her desire to be loved rather than lynched. In the face of crop failure, business foreclosures and fiscal finagling, Schub announces a forthright plan for financial recovery: a hoax to put the town on the map and bring in money.

THE MIRACLE While in one of her transient trances, Baby Joan (Jeanne Tanzy), the town's moppet mystic, approaches a large rock outcropping in the local park. When her strokings bring forth a fountain of water, Cora's cronies are on hand to proclaim, "A miracle! We're saved!" In the Miracle Song, the townspeople, egged on by Cora and Schub, decide to share the "non-sectarian" miracle with the world. When one helpful soul announces, "I feel better already," prosperity seems just around the corner. As a matter of fact,

Continued on next page

what is really around the corner of the rockpile is fellow-conspirator Chief of Police Magruder (James Frawley), pumping the water for the "miraculous" fountain.

During the years of decline only one institution has been in the dough—the local Cookie Jar, a sort of motel for mental misfits. Dignified but spirited Nurse Fay Apple (Lee Remick) shows up with 49 of her patients for the now-famous water cure. Comptroller Schub and Treasurer Cooley (Arnold Soboloff), selling tickets to gullible pilgrims with "special rates for minority groups," immediately realize the effect on business of 49 consecutive non-cures and refuse to sell tickets to the Cookies. An argument follows during which the Cookies intermingle with the "sane" pilgrims, from whom they are now indistinguishable. When Fay refuses to identify her charges, Schub arrests her, but she goes over the hill.

THE INTERROGATION *Doctor Detmold (Don Doherty), chief psychiatrist of the Cookie Jar, has come to town to meet his new assistant. He is unable to help Schub for, as he says, he wouldn't recognize his Cookies unless they were lying down on a couch. Handsome, energetic J. Bowden Hapgood (Harry Guardino) appears looking for Dr. Detmold's Cookie Jar, and Schub, relieved at the arrival of professional help, asks Hapgood if he can identify the Cookies by interrogating them.* "Simple," *announces Hapgood and proceeds to question everyone, placing each into either of two groups—"A" or "One"—according to his answers. But when they are all divided nobody can tell which group is sane and which insane—except Hapgood, and he's not telling.*

THE CELEBRATION Groups A and One parade through the town, each proclaiming its collective sanity: A-One March. The "epidemic of lunacy" brought on by the miracle continues with the arrival of a *very* French Lady From Lourdes (Lee Remick)—in a provocative dress, rhinestone slippers, dark glasses and flame-red hair—sent to test the miraculous water.

THE ROMANCE *For the moment, however, she curiously becomes more interested in Hapgood; and in* Come Play Wiz Me *they become better acquainted. In his hotel bedroom she invites him to chase her, promising she will let him catch her. As their love making becomes more torrid, she removes her wig and identifies herself as frigid Nurse Apple, dominated by Control and Order, unable to let herself go. Why, she is so inhibited she can't even whistle.* Anyone Can Whistle, *she assures herself, but the listlessness of her love making convinces them both that only a miracle can thaw her.*

THE PARADE Cora, delighted by the town's sudden prosperity, ending the persistent demands for her resignation, wonders why A Parade in Town isn't for her, as Hapgood is carried in triumph through the town on a psychiatrist's couch. Observes Schub: "If he weren't a psychiatrist, I'd swear he knew what he was doing."

THE RELEASE *In Hapgood's bedroom, Fay again hopefully dons her red wig but it fails to work its old magic. Hapgood urges her to forget responsibilities and set the Cookies free by tearing up the hospital records. He confesses that he is not a doctor at all. He is a new patient for the Cookie Jar, a disillusioned former statistician who could "prove" anything with figures. A victim of a society in which* Everybody Says Don't, *he is now happy to be a trumpeter who is a Pied Piper for lunatics. In a Ballet, we see how many of the Cookies "got that way"—parental or social pressures—and Fay agrees to free herself from Control and Order by freeing them. She destroys the records.*

THE CONSPIRACY Cora realizes she must rid the town of the Lady From Lourdes. She sees the foreigner's meddling as a threat to the miracle. Cora, Schub, Cooley and Magruder decide to turn off the fountain temporarily to get rid of the interloper and, blaming the failure on Hapgood, send him on his way too. I've Got You to Lean On, sing the conspirators.

THE CONFRONTATION *Hapgood and Fay discover the pump that makes the miracle work. Cora, still thinking Fay is the Lady From Lourdes, threatens to arrest her unless she leaves town. Fay rejects Hapgood's optimism in* See What It Gets You.

THE COOKIE CHASE Cora, Schub and Dr. Detmold now concentrate on rounding up the Cookies in a hilarious chase scene *(Ballet).* Since nobody can tell the sane from the insane, they simply round up the first 49 people they find. When Cora tries to throw the Lady From Lourdes into the Cookie Jar, Dr. Detmold recognizes her as Nurse Apple. Realizing that she can fight Control and Order no longer, Fay calls out the names of the Cookies: "Brecht, Herman, Dillinger, Myrna; Engels, David J.; Freud, Harriet; Ghandi, Salvatore . . ."

THE FAREWELL *Hapgood, feeling that his mission has failed, is packing to leave. Fay tries to persuade him that the world needs him: "We have more and know more, but still need miracles to make us happy." He wants her to come away with him, but she says her Cookies need her:* With So Little to Be Sure Of.

THE END The townspeople are making a mass exodus to the next town where a statue has been discovered whose heart is warm to the touch. Hapgood, sitting with his luggage by the hill from which the water once sprang, begins to blow his trumpet. As he goes off, people begin to follow him. Fay, realizing that *he* is her miracle, suddenly finds she can whistle and he returns to take her with him. As they depart the water issues once more from the hill, this time in token to the true miracle of love.

Anyone Can Whistle closed almost a decade ago. But it has remained very much a part of New York theatre talk since. Regrets that it seemed so much before its time, that the critics failed to understand the implications, the innovations. Sympathy for those who never saw it.

Those who did see it talk about the musical often. About the outstanding cast—Lee Remick, who had achieved stardom in television and films; English-born Angela Lansbury, who came from a long series of films to Broadway and after this performance achieved even greater stardom as the lead in such stage hits as *Mame;* Harry Guardino, noted stage and film actor; Gabriel Dell, who had begun his theatrical career as a juvenile delinquent in *Dead End* and scored in every phase of show business. And a meticulous and talented group of supporting players.

Stephen Sondheim has gained fame and honors for charting fresh territory in Broadway musicals—for giving it "a new lease on life." Leonard Bernstein, who wrote the music for Sondheim's lyrics for *West Side Story*, expressed the following opinion: "Steve is the most important force in the American musical theatre. He combines wit and intelligence in a very special way, and he's willing to take chances."

Sondheim has won Antoinette Perry Awards (Tonys) for Best Composer and Lyricist for Broadway musicals *Company*, *Follies* and *A Little Night Music* plus *Best Musical* for the latter.

Anyone Can Whistle has had no revivals. No movie. No foreign productions. This original cast album represents most of its existing life. So far.

But there is more. "Everybody Says Don't" is a much-performed song. And the title song has become a personal statement of Mr. Sondheim's, something the theatre world keeps alive.

The *Newsweek* story ended with this description. "Shortly after the opening of *A Little Night Music*, a gala benefit was held at the Shubert Theatre called 'Sondheim: A Musical Tribute.' After a glittering succession of performers had sung and danced their way through more than 40 Sondheim songs, Broadway's reigning music man sat down at the piano and, with tears streaming down his face, sang the title number from *Anyone Can Whistle:*

'Maybe you could show me how to let go, lower my guard, learn to be free
Maybe if you whistle, whistle for me.' "

Anyone Can Whistle was a commentary on our times, a philosophy, an entertainment. To be remembered.

—Mort Good

Anyone Can Whistle

Words and Music by
STEPHEN SONDHEIM

See What It Gets You

Words and Music by
STEPHEN SONDHEIM

See what it gets you. Trou - ble is, what - ev - er it gets, You

find that once you see

You can't stay blind.

blind.

Everybody Says Don't

Words and Music by
STEPHEN SONDHEIM

I've Got You To Lean On

Words and Music by
STEPHEN SONDHEIM

A Parade In Town

Words and Music by
STEPHEN SONDHEIM

Come Play Wiz Me

Words and Music by
STEPHEN SONDHEIM

With So Little To Be Sure Of

Words and Music by
STEPHEN SONDHEIM

There Won't Be Trumpets

Words and Music by
STEPHEN SONDHEIM